INSPIRATIONS

By Ilaya Gardez

Inspirations

First Printed in United Kingdom 2018

Published by Conscious Dreams Publishing

www.consciousdreamspublishing.com

ISBN: 978-1-912551-42-2

ACKNOWLEDGEMENT

Thank you God my creator for inspiring me to do my best and always being there for me.

Thank you to my role model Mabel Katz for being an inspiration to me and supporting me in my practice of Ho'oponopono.

Thank you to Annika Spalding, Writing Coach for believing in me and giving me the confidence and support through attending her writing with confidence workshop. By encouraging me to complete my book and get it published.

Thank you to my wonderful sister Kamela for being here for me on my self development journey.

Thank you to my friends Annika, Shirley and Deanne for giving me the encouragement to continue writing and offering their support.

Thank you to Daniella Blechner, Book Journey Mentor, Editor and Oksana Kosovan, Typesetter from Conscious Dreams Publishing. I am grateful for the support in my book journey to become a reality.

Thank you to everyone who reads this book.

"One of the greatest things about life is about being yourself and letting go"

LOVE

"Your heart is the compass of light

The beauty of life lies within us ♥."

Being the Real Me

I am walking with confidence and I talk assertively with clarity and I captivate my audience. My body language gives off positive vibes and I radiate beautiful energy. I lead by example and I show gratitude daily. I have an amazing circle of friends who are genuine and sincere and we support each other. I have built successful healthy relationships. I feel loved and valued wherever I go. I have grown as a person both personally and professionally. I feel special and unique and I have grown to accept myself. I'm doing more things I love and I feel happy. I am an enlightened soul. I am connected to the source and I am a powerful woman who is fulfilling her passion.

I love myself ❤

Dear Inner Child

Dear Inner Child,
Forgive me for not looking after you
Forgive me for not loving you
Forgive me for not listening to you
Forgive me for hurting you
Forgive me for giving you pain and suffering
Forgive me for neglecting you

Dear Inner Child,
I love you more than you know
I want to love and hold you in my arms
I want to stroke the top of your head with love
I want to show how much you mean to me
I want to give you all my love and attention
I want to be there for you always

Dear Inner Child,
Please let go of all that does not serve me
Please trust me to be your best friend
Please hold my hand and have faith in me
Please let's work together as a team
Please let's clear all the limiting beliefs
Please believe in me to help you

Gratitude

Gratitude is God's most wonderful gift
share it with all you meet and see how great things shift

Gratitude is a special feeling
actually giving you intense healing

Gratitude when felt from the heart
gives you an inner peace you don't want to part

Gratitude when beautifully experienced
creates ripples of goodness of a positive sense

Gratitude benefits all who choose to focus on the good
because great things then happen as they should

Gratitude transform your life from universal sights
giving attention to appreciation and rising to new heights

Having Love in Your Heart

Having love in your heart gives all you desire

Desires can come true when love is in your heart

Heart is God's gift of love and peace

Peace is the key to Happiness

Happiness is wonderful feeling

Feeling Joy is a blessing

Blessings come from gratitude

Gratitude opens doors to Abundance

Abundance is here and there

Here and there is God

God is Love

Love is felt in your Heart

Gratitude Changes Lives

Gratitude lifts you up to new heights
It takes you to new greater spaces beyond your eyes
Searching for good happens easier with gratitude as you cherish yourself and all that you have, you become a radar of light

Gratitude brings change in unbelievable ways
It changes your life because you choose to be grateful

Being grateful coming from a loving heart gives you your wildest dream
You become the real you
Full of love

Gratitude changes the way you feel. Choosing to focus on genuine appreciation you feel blessed

Gratitude brings you more blessings as you come from a pure heart.

The more you are grateful, the more you will be blessed
do it with love and experience miracles!

I Am Great

I am here now in the moment cherishing the time with
my loved ones, my family
I am one with myself loving myself and appreciating who
I have become

I am gracefully beautiful and growing into my true self by
connecting to the Divine, my higher self

I am full of so much love and feel I have so much to
give of myself

I am respecting myself and being kind to myself as I have
deep love for myself

I am a child of God and I deserve nothing but the best

I am pure as the ocean, fiery as the volcano, innocent as a
child, rich as Mother Earth, fresh as the air.

I am an eternal soul living forever in the golden age
of a woman

I am a strong, powerful, maternal, grounded woman who
touches the sky with her mystical aura

I am living an adventurous, blissful, magical, outstanding
life full of passion and purpose

I am attracting the true essence of who I am at zero being one with the universe

I am spirituality enlightened, glorifying the beauty within me and radiating an everlasting positive magnetism

I am great, a dynamic individual, born as human in this realm and showering my blessings upon this world

I Have Come so Far

I have come so far. My confidence has soared. I have high self-esteem. I am radiating beauty within me. I am loving myself freely. My luck has changed. My relationships are more meaningful. My friendships are genuine. I am wealthy within. I am full of gratitude and peace. I see my future bright and glowing with light. My life is a dream come true.

I have come so far. I feel completely satisfied. I have all the time for myself. I love being in nature. My life is surreal. Amazing moments are happening before my eyes. I feel God's presence liberating my soul. I am stronger and role model for many. I trust and believe in myself more than ever before. I have achieved greatness. My love life has transformed into a magical love story.

I have come so far. I have many wonderful supportive people in my life. I am enjoying precious moments of joy. I am making incredible wealth beyond my wildest dreams. I am letting go of what no longer serves me. My life is a successful journey. My spirituality brings me peace. My world is full of wonderful surprises.

I Love Me

I love me
I have what it takes
beautiful, special, unique. I'm the icing on the cake

I love me
I am generous and kind
glorious, sensational, genuine and with a precious mind

I love me
I have good qualities
mysterious, outstanding, marvelous, amazing royalty

I love me
I have so much to give
loveable, superstar, angelic and a brilliant life to live

Love is the Key

Love is healing my body and soul
From now on I feel whole

Money is coming to me from all avenues
I am fulfilled financially as I have revenue

Peace is evoking inside my every cell
My true self is awakening as well

Acceptance, gratitude, trusting and believing in
myself now
God almighty is giving his hand for me to hold WoW

Race, colour, creed, and gender no more
This is unity in motion as we are all one opening the door

Fate is bringing us together as our paths collide
Love devotion as we walk side by side

Blissful moments I share with loved ones from now on
I see I am lucky in many ways in front of the bright sun

Giving in no longer to temptations as my journey of self-
worth has just begun
Hatred no more for my fellow man just let bygones
be bygones

True happiness exists in the heart of man
Open yourself up to allow yourself as you can

Miracles do happen in this day and age
Look up to the sky and just see how is it possible to see the sun's rays

Every day is an adventure as we follow our heart
It doesn't matter where you are at just start

Positive thoughts lead to positive lives
Oh Holy Spirit, Father, Son and I have faith in myself as I will survive

Trusting in God will bring me all my desires
For he who has faith can overcome any fires

Be in a life of total honesty and trust
For the more you let go of expectations and it is a must

Rags to riches can be found
You too can have the golden crown

I Love Myself

In this life you have all you need
Just remember to be kind and do a good deed

Not being loved is no longer my moto
For I'm a beauty queen who is better than the lotto

I have within me the whole universe
As precious as I am since my birth

The golden key to the door you seek
It's not a mystery as you can open it as you
reach your peak

Mountains to climb are not difficult as you think
Live to your fullest then you've achieved what you want
in a blink

Roses to soul mates and lovers to sex
Accept the feeling of the human need without being vexed

Diamonds I can have too as I am worthy as I feel
Glad I believe in myself because I'm the real deal

Hocus pocus gobbledy goo, curses may exist
But I put my trust in God so there is nothing
I have missed

Angels exist on heaven and earth
They come in many forms to protect us

Heavenly father we ask for your helping hand
Your love has no boundaries as you are the Creator of everything on this land

Let yourself go to spiritual enlightenment
For you've now made it as you are heightened

Success is possible to all those who are willing to take it
Just remember put in the work and belief so you can fake it until you make it

I am the I on this planet and in this universe
Special, adored, honored, the one and only and diverse
another chapter another verse

I am the I ❤ Ilaya Gardez ❤

Love

Love is a healing energy. It can ignite passion in your soul
Love is full of trust and enlightenment. An open heart
gives without expecting anything in return

Love does make the world go round. With all the people
who show love this world will continue to shine

Love shows affection to your family to your partner and
children. Love has no boundaries it flows endlessly to keep
us together

Love shows signs from God. For God is true love never
ending bond which makes us whole

Love is in eyes of the soul as you can have deeper
connections. This is eternity were we came from and
will return

Love matters as it frees us from the chains of life. Your
life has purpose and meaning when you come from love

Love comes in form of gratitude as you cherish this
moment and what you have. Then love will give to you
more in the universe

Love Is

Love is a gift to mankind
God is peace and love and God is kind

Love is a gift that we can all share
God is love and love shows you care

Love connects us to our soul as we are all one
Precious love shines within as the bright sun

Love is a connection of the soul and spirit
Love gives us purity within as we fly in it

Love is felt in every creature, land and sea
It's only seen by the open-hearted and as it's free

Love is energy which connects us to all
You can forgive and release your pain and stand tall

Love is freedom, love is joy,
Love is transformational. Love is the real McCoy

Love is All Around Me

Love is all around me
Love is within me
Love is in my heart
Love is in my soul

Love is changing me for the better
Love can transform the world
Love is inspiration
Love is God

Love is a healer
Love is a blessing
Love is peace
Love is beyond understanding
Love is beautiful

Love is kind
Love is courage
Love is being true to myself
Love is being authentic
Love is powerful

Love is truth
Love is light
Love is the source
Love is believing in myself
Love is trusting myself
Love is accepting myself
Love is my higher self
Love is everywhere

Love Your Addictions

Addictions need to be loved to let them go
After all what you resists persists, don't fight the feeling
just go with the flow

Accept sex is a need don't push it away
You are only human so don't fight the feeling just accept
it's here to stay

God can help with your addictions just ask for his help
and so you can heal. Give in to His power because it's
the real deal

Many people go down a downward spiral wishing for things
to leave them
Come on wake up and see the light and cut out
the mayhem

Loving yourself is the greatest gift of all
Oh Father, oh Mother oh Universe feel the power of a
rising call

Addictions are resulting from unresolved issues
Stay in the present and let go of the old news

Love Yourself

Giving yourself time to be yourself is necessary to be successful
Only you can be your own best friend before you can have a best friend

When you truelly love yourself more love will come your way

The answers you seek are always inside you

When you are disciplined with yourself to be your best, deserve the best and expect the best then the best comes to you

Loving yourself opens doors to new possibilities which can transform your world

The greatest gift you can give yourself is love and then the love you desire will come to you

Be good to yourself and you shall receive goodness

Be kind to yourself and you will receive kindness

Loving Myself Again

Nobody likes me is a memory replaying
It's me focusing on my fears
and not loving myself

Self-care and self-love opens your heart
Focus on being in the moment instead of tearing myself apart

Loving myself again is happening here now
I'm amazing because I choose. Wow!

I let go and trust that all will be well
Here and now it's unto me if it's heaven or hell

Precious as a star shining so bright
I am becoming my true self of loving light

I love me and choose to be free
Living a joyous life full of ecstasy

Love, Love, Love is a beautiful word
It brings me to the most beautiful places I've ever seen or heard

My Heart

My heart, I ask you to stay open
and help me be the real me

My heart, I want to keep beating
and set me free

My heart, let my love shine
my beloved heart, oh mine, oh mine

My heart, unleash my deepest desire
for you are the Godly creation I admire

My heart, you help me live
you just keep pumping and all you do is give

My heart, you can heal so many wounds
without you it's not much of a life

My heart, when you close it's hard to get close to people
my dearest heart, I'm grateful to you my beating heart

My heart, I feel pain when I shut you out
I know this can cut like a knife

My heart, you are so pure and true
when you are loving nothing is impossible

My True Love

My true love is me
My true love is God.
My true love is peace
My true love is working with children
My true love is being funny
My true love is singing
My true love is dancing
My true is love Mother Nature
My true love is travelling
My true love is being free
My true love is seeing the light
My true love is Ho'oponopono
My true love is speaking the truth
My true love is living in the moment
My true love is living the dream
My true love is having children
My true love is getting married
My true love is writing
My true love is reading
My true love is living in harmony
My true love is wealth
My true love is appreciating beauty in nature
My true love is walking in the great outdoors
My true love is becoming one with God
My true love is being successful in business
My true love is loving myself
My true love is cherishing precious moments
My true love is enjoying great adventure
My true love is seeing the sea and walking on the beach

My true love is marrying the man I love and who loves me
My true love is taking opportunities which fulfill my soul
My true love is being spiritually connected to the Divine
My true love is being enlightened
My true love is being my authentic self

Self-Trust

Self-trust has been the hardest thing I have encountered until now because I am a believer
How do I trust others when I don't even trust myself?
Self-trust is vital for a successful business
Self-trust is needed to have meaningful relationships
Self-trust opens doors for you when you trust in yourself
Self-trust is having the faith that you can achieve anything beyond your wildest dreams
Self-trust is having a purpose and finding your own niche
Self-trust is believing in your capabilities to have the impossible
Self-trust is breaking down barriers and boundaries so you can live your life from your heart
Self-trust is giving yourself patience and kindness to follow your passion
Self-trust is the Mother of Hope, Love and Peace

"Self love is the number one key to self discovery which creates respect and trust in oneself."

BEING PRESENT

"Love and Joy can be experienced when we enjoy the moment that is before us."

The Story of my Life

There I lay on the grass feeling the warmth of the sunshine on my face and body. Just realized how far I have come in my life. Memories of my success allowing me to be inspired. I come from a place of love and see great qualities of people I meet. My body is transforming and I feel a sense of change for the better. The importance of present moment awareness allures me to freedom. Captivated by an inner calling to go all the way and meet my purpose. I have found myself and know I can trust myself. This is the time of self-acceptance, self-love and self-belief. Self-growth has taken me to a new era of deep gratitude for the soul. This has bought me now being the real, authentic me. The story of my life has ups, downs and the whirlpool of experiences which have made me who I am today. There is no right or wrong but a self-perception of reality. My inner guide has bought me this new age of being one with the Universe. The deep connection of spirituality is transcending me to my higher self. I found myself and the divine inside of me. This is the story of my life.

The Power to Change my Life

I have within me the power to change my life
My thoughts are my seeds
I can plant positive seeds or negative seeds

My thoughts can change my life
By intentionally focusing on the good and coming from
gratitude daily

My beliefs make me who I am
By asking God for help with healing and clearing, I can
internally become pure of heart

My beliefs can change for the better
By affirmations, focusing my attention on the positive and
choosing to be in the present

My life is my temple
It's up to me how I live peacefully coming from love
within my heart and soul

My life is a miracle
By coming from inspiration, connecting to my higher self
and the divine within me

Practise What You Preach

Practise what you preach
therefore don't just teach

Practise what you preach
follow your own path and make it unique

Practise what you preach
enjoy your moments don't keep grinding your teeth

Practise what you preach
live your dreams, fulfill your potential it's within
your reach

Practise what you preach
the here and now is all you have so don't delay or
dig a ditch

Practise what you preach
have a goal make it your own and have a pitch

Practise what you preach
if you want wealth take action and trust then you
will be rich

Practise what you preach
not criticize others just be humble and create a niche

Practise what you preach
don't give up on hope or yourself because God is always
here within reach

Letting Go

Letting go is the hardest thing I've done
facing my fears when I just want to run
not being serious, just wanting fun
loving myself has just begun

Letting go is letting go of expectations
not resisting what is without hesitation
learning to grow through meditation
working with others and collaboration

Letting go of what you resist
do it now before it persists
give into love before an opportunity is missed
take a chance, do you follow the gist?

Letting go takes courage and strength
only you can do it so be it hence
you have the key to look through the lens
stop living a lie of utter pretense

Letting go you transcend to a better place
Just peace, harmony and God's grace
join in love and be a special case
we are all one but not a single race

Being Strong

There I was sitting gazing at the sky
Who am I?
What am I here for?

Then the answers came to me
Be strong Ilaya you are here to be your best self
Don't let people bring you down

You are a strong woman full of charisma and magic
You have so much to give to the world
Your qualities your beautiful smile and gifted individuality

I've seen the signs
You were born to succeed
Here lies the power of your spirit. Face your fears and let your inner strength shine

Be the force for good
Allow the goodness within you to be used to serve others

When darkness comes to haunt you
Pray to the Almighty to hold your hand
Have faith and trust that all is well in the hands of God

Never give up on yourself even when you have nothing to give
Have hope that you can do anything and anything is possible

The greatest miracles happen when you let go
Amazing doors open in front of you when you let go of attachments

Be strong in your hardest times and know God is always by your side.

Amazing Things

Amazing things happen when you let go
Miracles happen all around us

Beauty is within our hearts if only we keep it open
God is the love we seek and makes us feel complete

Love is the true essence of who I am
I only need to look within to feel the love

Peace is a spiritual enlightenment of awakening
Express from open heartiness and see bliss

Present is joyous and momentous as there is no
past or future
Living in this moment is contentment

Gratitude brings more appreciation which in return
gives you more
Desires get fulfilled when you trust in the process

The Power of Gratitude

I am thankful for my life
I have so much to be thankful for
Thanking the trees that provide oxygen
Thanking the sun that gives us daylight
Thanking the Ocean for giving us the water to live
Thanking the human race for supporting each other
Thanking the moon and the stars for shining to give
us direction
Thanking my eyes, ears, mouth, hands, feet, my brain and
my body to help me move
Thanking all the wonderful lovely people who are
here for me
Thanking all my material possessions which make me feel
proud and blessed
Thanking the great leaders before me who provide
inspiration and hope
Thanking all the creatures who walk the earth from the
ants to the elephants
Thanking Mother Earth for letting us walk on her
Thanking Ho'oponopono for making me into the person
I am today
Thanking the heart for beating and keeping me alive
Thanking the fire to keep us warm in the winter
Thanking the snow to make Christmas magical
Thanking all the lovely food which tastes good and keeps
us content
Thanking myself for contributing to this planet

Being in gratitude changes lives

Take the Opportunity

Take the risks in life to change the way you think

Think like you are great already then you shall be

Be a believer in yourself and trust in the Universe

Universe is God and God loves you and me

Me, Myself and I are important as we are part of
the Creator

Creator Divine Source is here for us to connect

Connect with your inner soul and heart and all you desire
will come to you

You can be anything you desire because life is a miracle

Miracles do happen daily as you take opportunities which
are for your highest God

Life is Mystery

Life is a mystery and taking up history
Life is a mystery and full of love. Life is God's gift, it's a wonderful surprise, Life is a gift, it's marvelous and divine. Life is great, it can be full of love and hate. Life is a glorious way to alter your fate. Life is a transformation of miracles and light

Enjoying the Moments

Enjoying the moments is crucial to being happy
in the now
Life is precious. Tomorrow is promised to no one so let's
have some fun
Feeling grateful for what I have because love in my heart
is what will carry me to another endless path
Love is a feeling which gives you intense healing
God is a beautiful light giving us so much of what is right

Be Here Now

Stop comparing yourself to others
You are a gifted soul full of love and light

Stop undermining your ability to live your dreams
God the Creator can hold your hand to give you your
heart's desires

Stop blaming others for your misfortunes
You are a co-creator. Your thoughts and beliefs are seeds
which create your reality

Stop saying I can't do this or have that or the things
I would love to have
Put your trust and faith in the loving Father, Universe
and Divine

Stop belittling yourself. You are a strong, powerful human
being an essence of God

Stop carrying the guilt of shame.
Live in the moment and let go of what no longer
serves you

Stop saying you are not good enough
You have within you the power to conquer your fears, the
power to change your life and live with passion

Stop saying my past is haunting me
You can choose to live in the now and transform inside out with God's help
Stop saying I have nothing
Come from a loving place of gratitude and see the miracles of life daily

Now is the Time

Be here in the moment of truth
Being here now is love
Staying in the present is peace
Cherishing the moment is blissful
Staying connected to nature is being grounded

Loving yourself is true love
Giving what you want is kindness
Hugging with happiness is beauty
Seeing greatness is being open-hearted
Time spent wisely is a gift

Heart

Listen to your heart
You have the answers within you

Your heart is teaching you to be open
Come from love

The heart is a guidance system
Which allows you to come from inspiration

You can build relationships with your heart
You have a deeper connection

Listen to your heart
It's telling you what path to follow right for you

Heart of mine
I trust you will take me to my higher self

Your heart beats to make you breathe
It is giving you the miracle of life

The heart is a powerful source
It gives energy of love which creates peace

Heart of mine you transform my world
With your love I can heal myself

The Five Senses

I sat and viewed the world around. It's amazing how much beauty is around me. So much love, passion and wonderful views.
I walked amongst the trees and saw the most mesmerizing views of ecstasy which caused my soul to blossom into an avalanche of desire

I swayed into lovemaking, sex and experienced the union of soulmates come together

I talked and spoke of an everlasting inspirational piece of tranquility which came after I saw the sun shine on me

I heard a symphony of melodies which arose my heart to climax as the delightful music gave me intense pleasure and filled me up

I touched my lover with my heart and soul and he sang beautiful words of love into my ear. I surrender myself to my beloved and we bonded in spiritual bliss

I tasted sweet nectar from the ocean of love. I felt God's presence bestow blessings of joy. I let the light of God shine and gave myself away to the Divine

I saw the mountains and the valleys showing me the power of the universe. God came down to give His loving hand and lift up the spirits of mankind

Embrace and Accept Our Past

We must embrace our past not bury it
hide it or sweep it under the carpet
as it will come back and haunt us again and again
We have to accept it and send it love
Then move onto pastures new.

"Special moments occur when you just
enjoy the here and now
You can only be free when you choose to
be in the present."

LOVE AND RELATIONSHIPS

"The love you seek is already inside yourself."

Trust

Trust is a big motivator in determining what you do and become in your life

Trust can open doors for which you thought were closing

Trust can ignite self-belief and take you to the adventure of the life which you love

Trust can help you to fall in love with yourself so you are your authentic self

Trust is faith in action as you have self-trust, self-belief and self-love. This can make you invincible

Trust is taking good care of yourself by putting yourself first and saying no to things that don't serve you

Trust is believing in a higher power than yourself to fulfill your dreams

Trust is being in the present moment and creating a happy life for you by doing what you love

Trust is sharing your true self with others who love and respect you

Trust is building solid meaningful relationships by also starting with you

Trust is accepting what cannot be changed and trusting that better things are coming your way

True Essence of Who I Am

I have created things in my life because of my thoughts.

Me focusing on the negative things is closing the right doors for me

Therefore I have decided to not engage and take my life to great levels
I am believer of hope and taking the steps to grow dramatically

I can choose to let go and live in the present

I am seeing great changes within me which are allowing me to be my best self

I am doing things which are helping me to grow

I am being with people who are supporting my growth and personal development

I have seen a brilliance in my personality which is taking me to fall in love with myself

My New Life

My heart is full of fire
As I follow my desire

I am empowered to change my life for the better
Today, tomorrow and thereafter

I am realising my inner strength which has no end
As I embark on this journey to make amends

Doing some soul searching I came to the conclusion
My life is just a controversial illusion

Listening to my heart to move forward to pastures new
I must take risks which involves failure too

This is not the end, it's just the beginning
Fear is taking over but I want to be singing

It's all up to me which choices I make
As opportunities will come for me to take

Beyond the darkness lies the light
It all depends on what I focus on which I will see in sight

Anything is possible in this day and age
Just let go of the worry and see a new chapter on
a new page

My Transformational Life

There he is my handsome lover, friend and soulmate
All that I desire and full of love and a clean slate

He is charming, special, unique and one of a kind
Adorable, spectacular and sensational and fabulous just
like me. He's all mine all mine

His soul is connected to me, the spiritual bond is
unforeseen
He looks into my eyes and fills me with love and
such a dream

The magic between is sexually alive and heightened with
pleasure so mystified
What a man so perfect for me as I'm just being myself and
got nothing to hide

I've blossomed into a flower so pure and hot
Just completely loving myself whether people
like it or not

I thank God always for his love and blessings
Without him I would be not a single thing

I look in my eyes as I've fallen in love with myself
Beautiful, courage with the image of God I'm in
good health

This is the moment I share myself to the world my authenticity
A masterpiece, make-believe, real, so true and just perfect as I am free

I am confident and full of self-adoration as I see my qualities transform my world
Here I am so happy, at peace, achieving all my wildest dreams and telling my story untold

Just fully complete no need for another as I know see myself as my own lover
Fulfilling my life purpose I have everything I want as I take the steps and am no longer undercover

Freedom, success, financial stability has given me all I need
What a fortunate lucky life as I have planted the seed

I nurture myself with kindness and love as I've made a shift
Time is precious, unknown to man and the present is the perfect gift

I am Already the One

I came to a realisation that I wanted to be loved
but I am love

I realised I am searching for the one but I am the one

I want someone to complete me but I am already complete

I am looking to have the right relationship but it all
starts with me

I wanted respect and trust but I must feel it within first

I desire money and financial independence but I have all
the wealth I desire

I tried to please people but it didn't work

I want the perfect soulmate but I must become
what I desire

Be the Transformation You Seek

Helping yourself is a priority

Look after yourself first and everything will just fall into place

Be kind to yourself and respect your true hearts desires and it will come true

Be your own best friend and see you will make friends easily

Be love to yourself and love will come back to you

Be a good listener and people will want to hear what you have to say

Be your own lover inside and out and people will fall in love with you

Be the dream you want to accomplish and it will come true

Be the faith and believe in yourself and many will have faith and belief in you

Be the trust you seek and you will be trusted in return

Be the transformation you desire and you will see and feel the change in you

Be a gift with your heart and soul and your light will be a gift to those around you

Be the person you admire and that person will admire you

Be an inspiration to yourself and others will be inspired by you

The Essence of Who I am

There is so much beauty within me wanting to shine
I have come to self-acceptance which is now just fine

I have so much to give to the world. So much love, So
much passion, so much of me the real me to share myself
and my unique qualities
believing in myself, trusting myself and loving myself as
I treat myself with loyalty

It is remarkable to see I am a connection to the Divine, the
Universe, God and the Source. We are one. All connected
to each other.
Sister, brother, father, mother, son and daughter and all
relationships we are together

I feel tremendous passion and a sense of achievement of
how far I have come. God sees my qualities and wants me
to be me now.
I am seeing miraculous changes in myself and to me
this is wow!

I am now a believer of truth, a believer of love and a
believer in myself.
To come this far is all because I trusted my Higher Self

Everything I desire is already here. I no longer need to
search for anything.
This is the power of now as my heart continues to sing

All I want and want to be is within. God has given me the
power to choose my path.
Awakening to my higher self as I let go of death

I choose love, I choose God, I choose belief in myself and
the Divine
lighting the path for others as I continue to shine

I can see the light shining brightly giving me a sign to go
where God has the right path before me.
I am stronger than ever as I am now free

The path that brings me home to the real me, the
authentic me, the me which is my soul, spirit and source.
Gratitude, love and inner peace and happiness is the
right course

There, beneath the rainbow, is the essence of the real
me who is emerging fast and evolving into the gifted, the
loved and the one who is the I.
One with the universe, the creator I fly high

Love is in me, Love is around me and Love is my heart,
Love myself Love all Love God
Here's to the one and only God the creator of I. I applaud

Peace Of I

Friendship, Relationship, Love

Friendships, building relationships and love
How long it's taken me to trust myself and others
This journey of building relationships goes on and on

Where can I make friends with like-minded people?
I trust it will happen as I attract people like me

When is the time to settle down and be in love?
It can happen any time when you let go of expectations

Who are the people that can help me be a better person?
Only I have the key to my happiness as I fall in love with myself my world will change

What is the connection we have with others when our spirits and hearts meet?
It's a combination of chemistry when people can share their soul openly and just be themselves

Friendships

Friendship is about being you
Being real being true

Friendships is about trusting yourself and trusting
each other
Letting go of judgments and accepting one another

Friendship is being vulnerable and honest
just being in the moment and living in earnest

Friendships open doors to relationships which
having meaning
experiencing change and inner healing

Friendship can lead to a loving relationship
which is genuine, about giving and receiving

Friendship involves sharing your tears, fears and laughter
enter a world where you can live happily ever after

Friendship has so many beautiful colours of the rainbow
which come after a storm, rain or shine and gifts
what you sow

Friendships are being in and cherishing the moment
No matter who you are, you are important

Friendships are about giving each other compliments,
praising each other
and raising each other's vibrations

Friendships come from God in all seasons and reasons
To learn to grow and experience transformations

Friendships bring joy, peace and enjoyment of life
Whatever you wish and it comes true, celebrate with friends till the end of time

Love to Friendships ❤

I Have Fallen in Love with Myself

I have fallen in love with myself first
that's the only way even if it hurts

I have given my heart away now as I have allowed love in

I have started to trust again even though it's
causing me pain

I have taken the time to love what I see in the mirror
because there is only the here and now and nothing else

I have seen love in my heart and soul,
no point living a lie and digging yourself a hole

I have allowed myself to fall in love with the right person
loving unconditionally for no forsaken reason

I have allowed love into my heart
no more tearing myself apart

Put Yourself First

Help yourself first before you can help others
Be the love you seek before you want to be loved

See greatness in yourself before you expect the
greatness you want

Respect yourself first before you expect to be respected

Be yourself first before you want others to be themselves

Believe in yourself first before you expect others to
believe in you

Trust in yourself first before you expect to be trusted

My Husband is Here

I am in love with a great man who is so divine and he is all mine all mine
Handsome, clever and brilliant too
A strong special man is who

Generous loving amazing as well
He is wonderful and so meaningful

I have found a gorgeous man no like any other
He is my soulmate, twin flame and my lover

His positive aura fills me up inside
Oh Heavenly Father I want to be his bride

I'm captivated by his divine presence
Glorifying positivity of all essence

What a man who takes my heart
Oh my God I never want to part

I feel so complete having him around me
He is mystical, mysterious and as I share myself with he

I am true to myself because he is amazing
I'm open, honest as I love him. I'm his queen and
he's my king

My Vision

As I saw a vision of myself dressed in a beautiful
white gown
Looking beautiful wearing my flattering crown

Getting ready to marry the man of my dreams
My oh my! My life is a shining ray of beams

My eyes lit up looking into his glorifying and mesmerizing
eyes which captivated my soul
Being in this moment I am listening to my highest call

I came to realise the soulmate relationship exists and it's
not just a fantasy
This is so amazing and exciting as I live this reality

Seeing the appearance of my lover poured lust and sexual
arousal into my mind
Attracting this man who is one of a kind

This time it was a deeper enriching connection of the soul
Even before meeting him I became whole

Hearing his voice sent shivers down my spine of joy
I am feeling now he is the real McCoy

Touching his hand allowed the electrifying current
between us evolve into light
Taking the steps to move forward as I choose fight or flight

The lovemaking created the union of two souls
becoming one
Liberating each other into heavenly bliss as we
are now alone

Sensing, feeling each other's heartbeat made us
become closer
The sparks ignite as we let ourselves go in exposure

The sexual expectancy felt exhilarating as the passion
continued forever and ever
It feels like eternity as we say the ending is never

This is for real as I trust and allowed the relationship to be
full of love and commitment
Life is just perfect as our days of acceptance is full of
astonishment

Yes I've made it as I'm the happiest woman on earth
having found my twin soul, my true love, my best friend,
my lover and husband all in one
Being here now I have let go of my past as I no longer
want to run

My life is complete and I have accomplished my dreams
and my true heart's desires
I am fulfilled and content as I look at myself and
feel inspired

Relationships

Relationships make you, relationships break you
We have to take chances to fulfill our destiny

The relationship we have with ourselves is the most
profound and liberating when it is coming from love

Love opens doors to new possibilities of being our best
Best is all you can give yourself because you deserve it

It is a dream come true to hold you in my arms
Love is uplifting, inspirational and astounding

Relationships Can Work

It's all a mystery, meeting people and making friends
There's so much to learn to grow and ever changing bends

Being in love and have a meaningful relationship can work
You just have to open your heart become vulnerable and
let love in even if hurts

Building a friendship takes effort, trust and sharing
yourself to others
Now is the time to be authentic and be yourself even with
our mothers

Connecting with children gives you so much pride
Together as a team you have nothing to hide as you are
bonding with each other side by side

Falling in love with yourself is the best gift you
have for you
As you allow love into your heart then the love you have
is so true

You Are The One

You are the love of my life, my spiritual connection
So much beauty in you as you are a Godly creation

You are the love of my life, you make me feel complete
Having you near me, my heart skips a beat

I love you with my heart and soul
Oh my dearest I feel so whole

You are a dream come true. The kiss of your lips the caressing of your body makes me feel alive
Meeting you has been such a pleasant surprise

You are the greatest love, I trust you, believe you and I am allowing myself to open up to you
The opening of my heart is happening to let you through

You are a great lover, the sexual intensity and our spirits uniting when we make love
You take me to heavens above

You are my best friend with your kindness and charms
I just love having you in my arms

I can just be myself freely
I am in awe of you as I love you dearly

You are a blessing in disguise as I allow you into my life
This is the beginning of wanting to be with you as I am willing to sacrifice

You are brilliant, a great soul, who can make me
feel happy
Just having your company makes me feel like a
love-sick puppy

You are a great role model with your high self-esteem and
positive aura
Having you in my life must be my karma

You are a successful entrepreneur with your creative
talents and business mind
I no longer want anyone else as I leave the past behind

You are a blessing in disguise as I allow you into my life
With your sweet kisses and love I want to be your wife

You are wealthy, abundant and stable financially
Being independent I feel secure now absolutely

You are my soul and I am yours. I see us reincarnating
again and again until we meet again
We may have one life but let's live for today even though
we may thereafter feel the pain

You Came

You came to laugh with me yet you left me aside
What is happening with your mighty pride?

You are a dream in the making with your beautiful smile
My heart goes out to you as you walk along the Nile

You are a handsome man with your witty charm
Oh my oh my I feel so good when you hold my arm

You are my best friend, a lover and a soulmate
This is a miracle how I met you at the fete

You look amazing and mesmerizing
My body, when it sees you, is dancing and singing

You a red rose with thorns so sharp
Let's play the music and the harp

You sang such a lovely song even the birds enjoyed
Listen, I will never get annoyed

You rang the bell on my wedding day and proposed the day before
This has been my wish granted as we are husband and wife forevermore

You listened to me cry as I wept alone
Oh my lovely you have a beautiful cologne

You gave me love when I called your name
My darling you could never bring me shame

"Fill your heart with love of oneself and you can change the world as you change everything changes."

SPIRITUALITY

"To love yourself means you love God."

Spiritual Journey

This is an amazing day full of glorious wonderful
compliments, kindness and exhilarating success
My day is full of love, pure bliss and excitement causing
me to blossom into a flower

I'm loved beyond belief because I love myself
My day is giving signs that I am connected to the Higher
Source. Therefore I am the Universe

My belief in myself has magnified because I am a piece of
God therefore an essence of a Goddess
Every day is special to me because I make it so
The wonders of the 7 worlds exist in me because
I am the world

Beautiful exists in my life because I am beautiful
Day by Day I create my own destiny as what
I focus on grows

My Lord, God, Angel the Higher Source believes in me
therefore I believe in myself
I deserve the best because I am the best

I love myself because I am love so the love I seek is within
me Day by Day, I grow into magnificence of my true being
because I am worthy of the light I shine

Every day I see brilliance in this world because I choose a
better way for me
I believe that all that I am is because God loves me so.
I choose to be with God

God

God does exist and miracles do happen
The glory of God is a light shining so bright
You can have, be, do anything with Gods blessing and
reach amazing heights

Our heavenly Father gives us hope in troubled times
Beautiful loving God is here to shine
God is a star who travels through endless time in all
galaxies for eternity so sublime

God is a master, Creator and powerful beyond all
Giving his love and support through the long haul

God, Divine, Universe special and sweet
No one on earth is ready to take on His seat

God is the sun, moon, stars, galaxies, planets, mother
earth, sea, fire and air
He is magical, miraculous, mystical and lucky is the one to
be in his glare

Ho'oponopono

I am the I

I am the creator of my life with my thoughts, deeds, words and actions
This is where I am 100% responsible for myself

Just by saying thank you, I love you consistently I can transform my life.

Clean, erase, let go and trust

As I practice the cleaning, I will change so will my outside circumstances change. It starts from within

Loving myself will allow the right relationship to come to me

By cleaning, I will attract the right relationships to enter my life

So I must clean to change by self-transformation everything changes

Blue solar water will clean away my bad habits, addictions, fears, insecurities and bring me back to zero

When my heart is open then I can give and receive love

Ho'oponopono will open the doors for me which appear to be closed, the right people, opportunities and situations will emerge for me

Moment by moment, I am choosing to let go and trust or hold onto attachments and expectations

Peace of I

My Spiritual Path Ho'oponopono

Ho'oponopono is a dream
My heart, my soul I am ready to clean

Ho'oponopono allows me to be at peace with trust
Cleaning, cleaning, cleaning consistently is a must

Ho'ponopono is a gift from God
The love of self is important especially on your tod

Ho'oponopono is creating self-change and transformation
Ever evolving mankind into self-adoration

Ho'oponopono is setting me free from me
As I'm a creation of infinity

Ho'oponopono is clearing away memories which obstruct
my unique path
It's building a bridge to connect with the higher self after
the aftermath

Ho'oponopono is God's answer to a prayer
It gives us hope when we are in despair

Ho'oponopono is a shining white light
Giving us belief and trust in the almighty in the
darkest night

Ho'oponopono is a rainbow so beautiful to see
Miracles it magnifies and bestows blessings for you and me

❤ I am a Goddess ❤

I see beauty in my heart and soul. I am a Goddess so
powerful and strong
With my inner light I shine, no need to prove
anyone wrong

I see beauty and strength in others. It's such an amazing
time for me
With my self-confidence booming and self-love igniting

I am following my true heart's calling. My passion is
unleashed and I am free of the past
My life is changing so drastically as time moves so fast

I have let go of all that no longer serves me for my highest
good. Greater opportunities are coming my way
So now finally my spirit is free day by day

I open my arms to my passion and let my light
shine through
Being here now is a dream come true

Amazing transformation has taken place in my life letting
me be the real me, genuine, authentic, humble, more
open to awakened relationships with a loving heart
The Goddess within me is a creation of the one and only
godly part

This is my time to be awakened and I see many of my
deepest heart's desires coming true. God loves All
Let's follow the path as we hear God's call

I am Light

I am light
Shining so bright
I am light
Soaring into great heights
I am light
giving hope to all in sight
I am light
loving, kind and full of delight
I am light
giving a sign is right
I am light
so powerful and strong heading outright
I am light
lighting up the night
I am light
Truly magical, mystical twilight
I am light
the wonder of calling God tonight
I am light
full of love and holding on so tight

I am the I

I am sensational
I am beautiful
I am amazing
I am captivating
I am the greatest
I am loved
I am kind
I am powerful
I am a child of God
I am sweet-hearted
I am the oceans so strong
I am the earth so courageous
I am the sun giving the warmth
I am the moon shining the light
I am the stars so bright
I am the air giving energy to breath
I am the God within sending love

I am the Miracle

I believe in miracles because they exist
Enter my heart and hear its beating persist

I believe in myself because I am worthy
Living right here makes me crazy

I go into the dramas of my mind and engage in
the thoughts
I always have a choice where I put my attention because
nothing is mine or bought

I release my emotions and let go of what is not me
This is the only way I can set myself free

I am brilliance of everything that exists in the universe
I therefore coincide with my own verse

I take my emotions and feelings and let them go
This is my life, that's why I am who I am so

I am the One

I am the one
It's all in me
I am free

I am the one
Courageous, bold and strong
loving, kind and bursting with song

I am the one
beautiful, sensational a spiritual being
full of passion, integrity truth is all I am seeing

I am the one
connected to source, showing gratitude and inspiration
making my dreams a reality and my aspirations

I am the one
free from attachments, living in the moment
giving all I can to as 100 percent

I am the one
loving my soul for all I am worth
Protected, nurtured and respecting Mother Earth

I am the one
No need for another as I'm a masterpiece
devoted to self-love and allowing doors to open
with my keys

I am the one
Created by God, gifted, talented and born as a miracle
Being my authentic self, giving my best, healing myself and reaching my pinnacle

Peace Begins with Me ♥

Take good care of yourself
Love yourself
Be kind to yourself
Be proud of yourself
Do things that make you happy
Do things that you love
Trust yourself and the Divine/God/Universe

People can Change the World

The beautiful rainbow gave me a humbling experience
The power to relate to people is a must
Serve others and you will feel fulfilled
Follow your passion and you will love what you do
Give love to receive love
Smile to people even if you don't feel like it
Show kindness and appreciate the good people in your life
Make time for your loved ones
How you speak to and treat people shows a lot about you
Keep your heart open to come from love
Meaningful relationships heal the world
Be true to yourself and be you
Real friends will accept you as you are
Love yourself and the love you want will come to you

Joy Peace Love Happiness

Joyous moments only happen when you trust and let go

Give yourself credit for your achievements and praise

God's beauty is always around us as we are part of
the universe

Having good health is always such a wonderful surprise

Success is given to those who truly believe in themselves

Dreams can come true if you are willing to do what it
takes to pay the price

♥ Love yourself as a body and soul as well as a spiritual being ♥

Your purpose in life is to be at peace no matter what

You have the power to transform and change your life within you

You have all the answers you are looking for within

God is always here and hears you calling

You are an infinite being with so much potential

Everything you desire is already here

God loves you more than anyone

You have a power within which is invincible

Every door that opens lights up to give you hope

Hope is the answer to your prayers

Focus on putting yourself first and everything will be ok

People of great power are great souls. You are a great soul and have great power

You are one with God

God is me. God is You. God is everything

I am the I. Peace of I

Praying

Praying is a natural way to call God. It takes us to test our belief in the Almighty

Praying can bring us joy when we trust and have faith in our Lord, Divine, the Universe, the Creator

Praying can make us stronger when we take chances to better ourselves by keeping the faith

Praying can make our dreams come true with persistence and faith

Praying works when we let go of expectations and trust that God will give us what we need

Praying opens doors to heaven on earth so we can live in peace and joy

Praying can teach us to be our best and reach our potential by believing in ourselves and God

Praying can show us miracles when we truly put all our faith in our Lord the Creator

Praying can cause us to change in ways beyond what the human eye can see as we are all one with the universe

Praying and asking for help from God gives us the guidance we need because God is always here

Truth Seeker

Who is God?
The Creator of Life
The Creator of the Soul

God is Truth
God is Love

The Universe is Infinity
The Universe is beyond all expectations

Life is a heart-beat of the Earth
Life is the breath we take

Mother Earth is caressing us with her love
Mother Earth has given birth to all that is here

Spirit is the soul within us
Spirit takes us to the Godly realm

Peace is the quietness of the mind
Peace is felt within the heart

Love is endless
Love is gratitude

Finding Myself

Here I am living here. Who am I?
Feeling lost in a crazy world

Always wanting more not being true to myself
What do I want? My life is a mystery

Where am I going? Am I happy with myself?
I am who I am

I must be kind to myself
I can do things that make me happy

I have what it takes
I can climb any mountain
I can have, do or be anything

The world is my Oyster and I am my world

Love life bliss golden moments are here now
Nothing to wait for to come true
Let God be your torch and have the trust he will guide you to your path

God speed

You Are the Co-Creator

You are the co-creator of your own life

You have within you your heart's wishes fulfilled

The greatness you seek is already within you

God the truth is hearing your prayers

Keep the faith and truth knowing that God gives you what is right for you. ❤

The real beauty in life is love

Love yourself and you will be the real you

Be the real you and give your best in all you do

Do good for others and expect nothing in return

Return to your Higher Self and know God is within you

You are an amazing soul who is transcending to greatness

Greatness only happens when you give from the heart

Your heart is the most precious gift in life

Life is about living your purpose to your fullest potential
Potential is achieved by working hard by following
your passion

Passion is a feeling which occurs when you love what you do

Do what you love and the rest is history

History is your past that is the story of your life

Life is breathing in the moment and feeling blessed

Blessed are the ones who give themselves to God

God is the greatest creator of life, soul and the heavens above

Above lies truth of why we are here

Here is the now the present is all we have

Have faith in yourself and God and see the miracles happen

Your Soul

Your soul is your inner light
Your soul is the truth
Your soul knows your heart
Your soul is connected to God
Your soul is Divine and it shines
Your soul is open to the higher power
Your soul will direct you to all that is good

Your soul will open doors if you allow it
Your soul is freedom when God is here
Your soul is beyond your wildest desires
Your soul will exist till eternity
Your soul is great
Your soul is giving you the answers you seek if you only listen
Your soul is pure and it will always be here

Listen to your soul and transform your life.

Soul Searcher

"You are the everlasting truth of love and within you is the entire universe."

EMPOWERMENT

"Self belief ignites passion which allows you to fulfill your life purpose."

I Have the Key

I have the key to transform my world

I have the key to my heart

I have the key to open doors of opportunities

I have the key to peace

I have the key to let God in

I have the key to love

I have the key to all possibilities

I have the key to be open and honest

I have the key to wisdom

I have the key to health

I have the key to light up my world

I have the key of choices

I have the key of wealth

I have the key of forgiveness

I have the key to faith and trust

I have the key to believe in myself

I have the key to being in the moment

I have the key to celebrate myself and my uniqueness for
I am the key to my life

Anger is my Friend

Anger is my friend. How funny is that?
What you resist persists and that's a fact

Anger is my enemy. No that can't be true
If I think this thought, I must have gone barmy too

Anger is burning up inside me but I choose to let it go
My heart still wants to come out and play even if I am feeling low

Anger is a sensation; an emotion of bottled up feelings
Maybe it's time to be honest with yourself so you can go through a healing

Anger is telling you to put yourself first
Doing things to please others only hurts

Anger can erupt hatred inside of you
Do whatever it takes to let the inner light shine through

Anger, if it continues and not dealt with correctly,
Will make you ill. Just work on yourself perfectly

Anger is my friend but only for the moment
For I choose peace which will make me content

Change your Life

Changes can and do happen when you are ready to change

Change is in the inner to experience the outer change

Change is good when you let go

Change often takes you to a new direction

Change can be for the better. When you do your best, things will change for the best

Change only occurs when you change

Change can give you a new lease of life

Change can transform your world

Change is a beautiful experience when it comes from the heart

Change of old habits can create miracles

Change is helping me to get out of my comfort zone

Change is accepting what you can't change and changing what you can

Change is allowing me to be my true authentic self

Change is taking me to a new dimension

Change can be wonderful when you allow the right things to happen

Courage and Fear

Face your fears of achieving what you want

Face your fears to live the life of your dreams

Have the courage to follow your heart's path

Have the courage to open up to have a meaningful relationship

Do what it takes to overcome your fears of success

Do what you must to be happy and let go of your fears

Allow courage to be a master to accomplish your goals

Allow courage to go in the direction living with passion and purpose

Good and Bad

Anger results in conflict
Conflict creates hatred
Hatred lead to revenge
Revenge can kill

Love creates peace
Peace is light
Light is within
Within us is God

Jealousy is bitterness
bitterness is discontentment
discontement is part of your feelings
feelings are emotions

Good is being happy
Happy is gratitude
Gratitude comes from the heart
Heart bears our soul

Religion causes controversy
Controversy leads to arguments
Arguments create war
War is destruction

Spirituality is enlightenment
Enlightenment is within our souls
Souls live forever
Forever is our journey

I Have a Choice

I take steps to move forward. Peace begins with me
I have a choice where I put my attention
I have a choice where I focus my mind
I have choice who I spend my time with
I have a choice where I want to be
I have a choice what I want to become
I have a choice what I do with my time
I have a choice to be myself
I have a choice to do what I love
I have a choice to be here now

I have a choice

I Have What I Want

My love for you is true
I love you more you will know

My life is a true miracle
I see amazing things happening everywhere

My beauty is skin deep
I am owning my unique qualities

My family care about me
I have the love and support I need

My strength is coming out
I am allowing myself to overcome my fears

My soul is enriched with a spiritual power
I feel enlightened and feel at peace

My Inner child is bonding with me
I have connected and feel we are getting closer

My relationships mean the world to me
I am building meaningful, healthy ways to work
with others

My job is what I love
I have a purpose and passion

My finances are rich
I am wealthy and abundant and free

Ilaya is Believing in Herself

I believe in myself
I have so much to give to this world
I Ilaya Gardez am a manifestation of the Divine
I can choose how I live my life
I can transform my world
I can change my fate

I am Love
I am Lust
I am anger
I am Peace
I am Blissful
I am Humble
I am the Seeker of Truth
I am Successful
I am a failure
I am an enlightened soul
I am Light
I am the cosmos
I am living the dream
I am Superwoman
I am nobody
I am a weak mortal
I am Nothing
I am Zero

Ilaya is the universal connection to God

Ilaya the Great

Ilaya is a generous soul

Ilaya is loving and wonderful

Ilaya is positive and inspirational

Ilaya is kind hearted and beautiful

Ilaya is loved and wanted

Ilaya is a great woman

Ilaya is strong and courageous

Ilaya is transforming for the better

I'm Learning

My experiences of life have taught me to trust and believe in myself. I am living the life of my dreams.
I am learning to walk the talk. My confidence is growing.

I'm learning to grow to be my best self.
Even though it hurts I am choosing to do my best.

I'm learning to work with people to have meaningful relationships. Even though its hard work I am choosing to grow as a person.

I'm learning to love and accept myself. Even though my heart aches from the pain of growing

I'm learning to be more disciplined. Even though I've found it hard to adapt to change and old habits come back.

It's My Choice

Even though I have moments of feeling upset, fear, worry, sadness and anger, I have the choice to be free It's all unto to me.

I can choose to be happy
I can choose laughter
I can choose sadness
I can choose being broken
I can choose to be in the moment
I can choose to be in the past
I can choose to let go
I can choose to react
I can choose to enjoy what I have
I can choose to be grateful
I can choose to look at lack
I can choose to be positive
I can choose to be negative
I can choose to live in the darkness
I can choose to go in the light
I can choose God
I can choose the Devil
I can choose to do my best
I can choose not even try
I choose to fulfill my destiny
I can choose to give up
I can choose to enjoy my life
I can choose to be depressed
I can choose success
I can choose failure

I can choose to be a winner
I can choose to be a loser
I can choose Love
I can choose hate

It's my Choice

Me Being Me

I am the I
Hating myself is burning me up inside
creating a fire with flames which are defeating my pride

Anger inside me is blowing up causing hate and war
But this is my story so far and there's more

Not loving myself completely comes back to haunt me
As the past is causing me pain and I'm not free

I have a choice where I go as my life is a strain
So much positivity if I focus on the good vibes, got so much to gain

Living a lie I realise I am not free from my past
As family, relationship memories keep replaying so fast

Giving into fear is easy as pie
Only I can be courageous and survive

No one can help me be my authentic self
This is why it's important to let go what is on the shelf
Peace of I

My Habits

My habits are causing me pain as I am choosing to feel
the strain

My habits are hurting me deep inside
As I continue this path I will have to swallow my pride

My habits are breaking me as I have allowed them
to take over
They continue to bother me as I hide for cover

My habits are not good
As I've hurt other people not kept my heart open
like I should

My habits of not cleaning has left me behind
So many missed opportunities which I can't find

My habits I can change because I can control
What happens in me to before I grow old

My habits are affecting my subconscious mind
Many difficult situations are created by me as I unwind

My habits are formed with me repeating my behavior
I take responsibility for this my Saviour

My Life Uncovered

Here I stand all alone feeling lonely once again
The pain of my past haunting me again and again

Not changing and accepting myself has come as a strain
Living not my fullest potential is driving me insane

Feeling lost and confused I'm singing in the rain
This very moment is such a pain

Repeating old patterns along the country lane
This is my life of hallucinations is making me
mentally insane

Just living in the here and now is brightening up again
I am choosing to be happy once again

Not having a lover to hold is causing me pain
But I trust in God so I have so much to gain

Growing stronger I choose to remain
Remembered for my courage and authenticity
I am alive once again

Not Feeling Good Enough

I am the I
Not feeling good enough cannot be ignored
You must honour the feeling and let it go or you will be just bored

Not feeling good enough is a barrier that you must succumb
There will be obstacles along the way but you must not play dumb

Not feeling good enough is comparing yourself to others which is not good
You must love and accept yourself and stop pleasing others to fit in the neighborhood

Not feeling good enough is not living from the heart
Follow your own unique path and just make a start

Not feeling good enough you miss what is rightfully yours
If only you just believe in yourself and trust in the process to open the doors

Not feeling good enough is you giving up on you
Come on now. This is the opportunity for you focus on you and you will certainly shine through.

Peace of I

Not Loving Myself

Not loving myself is causing me pain
Here I go again

Not loving myself is such a shame
Hurting myself and playing a game

Not loving myself I'm killing my self-esteem
Hurting my inner child as if we are not a team

Not loving myself because I am choosing the negative
Living this life I have no other motive

Not loving myself I focus on the past
Memories replaying on and on so fast

Not loving myself I am creating fear and sadness
This world of mine there is all but madness

Not loving myself I go back and forth repeating
negative patterns
If only I let go of expectations and resisting temptations

Not loving myself I can decide to focus on the good
As I continue to work on myself practice, practice,
practice as I should

Words

Fool, idiot, stupid, are mere words of the ego
Our inner child is guiding us and wants us to follow
inspiration

Brave, courageous, open and *honest* are words
coming from love
Be bold follow your dreams and come from inspiration

Beautiful, *kind*, *wild* and *free* is being your true self
Come let your inner light shine in this world

Jealousy, *hatred*, *revenge* and *fear* bring turmoil and pain
Be here now not comparing yourself others

Peace, *bliss*, *adventure* and *enjoyment* are all you need
Just material possessions cannot fulfill your needs

Bitterness, *anger*, *lust* and *greed* cannot give you
peace of mind
All you want is to live your true potential and leave the
past behind

Words Words Words

Words Words Words are important when used wisely
Making any situation transcend positively

Liberation
Exhilaration
Transformation
Manifestation

Words Words Words are so beautiful to me especially the positive ones that set me free

Beautiful
Magical
Mystical
Special

Words Words Words are amazing to hear
Especially the ones that help you let go of fear

Hoping
Dreaming
Living
Sharing

Words Words Words are uplifting my spirit
They rise me up and give me credit

Enlightenment
Empowerment
Transcendent
Evolvement

"Believing in oneself is lighting a candle in the dark and it will continue to shine and burn as long as you look after it."

MOTHER NATURE

"Beauty is always around you just need to look within to see it."

On the Beach

There I lay on the beach allowing the sun's heat to warm my face and body
Glowing, flourishing and just being nobody

The sand caressing my skin
The sun's bright rays giving an exotic experience; this is heaven in every season

I walked along the seashore and watched the waves moving in motion
Hearing their roars of movement along the seashore soothing me like a lotion

Feeling the sand on my naked feet made me connect deeper to my higher self
Love never ending just being me my true self
Just feeling utter bliss, devotion for my unique self,

At peace in love with who I have become
Oh mighty God I am stunned

The cooling of the sea water making me stop and listen
Feel a cleansing process has just begun as though I've been christened

The lovely sea breeze just captivating my soul
What an experience! My life is full of fun, sun and enjoyment and making me whole

Being in this precious moment is so divine

Listening and seeing Mother Nature I am feeling on
cloud nine

Never wanting this experience to end of being my true
self the essence of who I am
Oh beloved Father, Spirit, Divine Creator, Universe you
are the one

This is my Life

As I walked alongside the beach, I looked at how far I have come. Wow! What a confident woman full of joy and passion. Seeing myself in the mirror, I see a courageous, sensual, beautiful and gracious woman who loves to help others. I have reached new heights beyond my capabilities. Even I don't recognise myself. I am just going from strength to strength. I am radiating a positive energy which captivates people's hearts. I have an inner drive to be more, do more and lighten up my path. The people surrounding me take me to another dimension of self-love. I am blessed in many ways having found great peace, success and enjoyment in my life. This is what I call life.

Anything is Possible

Anything is possible living in God's eyes
Anything is possible it will take you by surprise

Anything is possible in this day and age
Anything is possible without being a sage

Anything is possible seeing miracles unfold
Anything is possible when your story is told

Anything is possible when you believe inside
Anything is possible when you don't hide

Anything is possible coming from faith and trust
Anything is possible when you say I must

Anything is possible when you just let go
Anything is possible when you sow

Anything is possible when God is here
Anything is possible when you let go of fear

Anything is possible being here now
Anything is possible when you let go of how

Be Like a Tree

Be like a tree so honest and true
Blowing in the wind through and through

Be like a tree special, unique not care in the world
Opening up to all and giving a twirl

Be like a tree grounded and connected to source
Being in the moment and at peace and just following the right course

Be like a tree loving and respecting mother earth
Living its purpose and doing what it's worth

Be like a tree standing tall in all seasons
Not comparing itself to others for any reason

Be like a tree happy and proud
Just being itself and speaking out loud

I Choose my Path

I have a choice in all I do
So many paths before me
I can choose to let go and trust or I can choose to hold on to the past

Travelling to many places appeals to me
I can choose to stay here or go to the unknown outside my comfort zone

Mediating and walking in nature is my love
I can choose to stay stuck or go with the flow by following my inspiration

Helping others brings me joy
I can choose to be selfish all the time or come from a loving and giving place

Working with children feels like my passion
I can choose to work in jobs I don't want or follow my heart to living with purpose

Eating foods which are healthy make me feel good
I can choose junk food or I can eat natural foods which originate from Mother Nature

Doing exercise energises my body
I can choose to sit and watch TV all day or I can get motivated to get up and feel vibrant and alive

Singing brings out the best in me
I can choose to use my voice for no meaning or I can sing to my heart's content and feel fulfilment deep within

Dancing feels amazing and uplifts me
I can choose to watch others enjoy themselves or I can push myself to move with the music and follow the rhythm of my heart

It All Matters

The sunshine is brightening up everyone's day
Making room for new exciting ways

There are many ways you can change your life
Be happy now then you will find the perfect
husband or wife

Be a good wife to a good husband and have a soul mate
relationship
It all matters because true love for your beloved involves
the right partnership

Having the right partnership makes all the difference
Everything you always wanted is a matter of preference

It's Funny

It's funny how anger can dissolve
It's funny how the world evolves
It's funny how I am human
It's funny how I am a woman
It's funny how we walk, talk and move
It's funny how we sleep, weep and groove
It's funny how we live and die
It's funny how we laugh and cry
It's funny how there is day and night
It's funny how there is dark and light
It's funny how there is Devil and God
It's funny how there is cat and dog
It's funny how we are born young as female or male
It's funny how we grow old and fragile
It's funny how we are lazy and disciplined
It's funny we are saints or have sinned
It's funny how there is gratitude and selfishness
It's funny how there is tidy and there is mess

The True Essence of Life

Here I was living a lie not seeing the real me

Feeling lost in a world of illusion

Dreaming my life away wanting things to be different

Until there it was the truth of who I was. The answer lay right in front of my very eyes. I became the true essence of who I am today. There He was. God the inspiration that is within me even in my darkest hours. God the one who created me and made into the authenticity, the core of my heart and soul.

Now I came to realise no man nor woman can give me what I need for all I want is here inside of me. The happiness I seek is within coming from a loving place. When I nurture myself, my inner light shines and feel a sense of belonging. The sun is allowing me to see greater things and the wonders of life come alive. Mother Nature protects and loves to her limitless capabilities until we see who she is really. The planet we live on is full of curiosity and deep desires of the unknown. This is the true essence of life. Find oneself and find God

Listening to Myself

I am the I
I walked onto the rainbow and seen the most beautiful light
As I hugged a tree I felt God came to rescue me
When I walked along the sea shore my mind wandered onto the sunset
I looked in the mirror and saw a lion roar
I heard a dark voice but I chose not to listen
I felt the earth move as I swam in the sea
The fragrance of the air humbled me

There it was the Light

All my life I was searching for the light. Hoping it would shine on me

But not realizing the light was always there because I couldn't see it

It was a ray of sunshine in an empty street
The light gave me hope in a dreary situation.

I allowed the light to guide me to pastures new and see myself as I am

The light made me see it's not all doom and gloom as I dwelled on its brightness to pull me through

Even in my darkest hour I chose to shine with the light beside me the sun gave me hope

I saw the light bring changes in my life as I trusted and believed it was time for me to shine

Live Life Love

Love is beauty. Beauty is gracious.

Gracious is peace. Peace is God.

God is Great. Great is the Ocean.

Ocean is Powerful. Powerful is I. I am the I

I is the Universe. Universe is eternity.

Eternity is Unlimited. Unlimited is the galaxy.

Galaxy has the planets, Planet Earth is Here.

Here is the moment. Moment is the present.

Present is alive. Alive are us. Us are the human beings.

Human beings have souls.

Souls have the spirit. Spirit lives forever.

Forever is now. Now is a gift. Gift is Love

The Growth of Life

The flower with all its beauty and glory
Opened up into the woman I am today

The caterpillar as it grew into the most beautiful butterfly
I became such a powerful authentic inspiration to myself

The lava as it flows in the volcano
I erupted and released all my inhibitions and aspirations to
live the life I have

The waves as they cross the ocean
I allowed my confidence to grow and develop into
going with flow

The candle as it shines the light
I too am letting my inner light shine so I can ignite to be
my true best self

The tree as it grows from mother earth
I let myself form roots so I can be centered and grounded

The air as it moves freely without a care
I connect with nature and breathe to be in the moment

Nature is Beautiful

The happiness you seek is deep within your heart and soul
Nature is beautiful
I love the trees and hearing the leaves lay on the
floor in autumn
The natural colors of autumn make me feel alive
Nature welcomes me into the woods, the forests, canals,
the hills, the lakes and ponds
I love nature walking alone in the midst of hearing the
wind whispering in my ears
I talk to the trees with love in my heart and get answers to
everything I ask
Nature has all the answers as is one with the Universe
I see the scenic landscapes the beauty of my surroundings
Nature tells me all I need to hear
I touch and hug a tree and wow inspiration comes through
as I have connected to my roots again
Nature speaks the truth as it calls my name to surrender
to this very moment
I walk and see, hear, speak and touch the present moment.
Nature is captivating me with her beauty

Another New Day is Dawning upon us

Another new day is dawning upon us inspiring us to
change for the better
Another new day is dawning upon us telling us to be
a go getter

A new life is upon the horizon lighting up our path
through the darkness
A new life is in front us wanting us to take the
opportunities that are given for us to harness God the
almighty has his hand on our head blessing us with his
tranquil presence

God the Almighty is giving his shoulder for us to cry upon
which allowed us his everlasting essence
Glad I have woken up to a new way of living

Glad I have fallen in love with myself and learning giving

Understanding Myself

I lay in my bed contemplating the meaning of life.
The answers came to me with the presence of God

As the leaves dropped on the floor from the tree, I walked and saw an amazing transformation take place within me. I realised the importance of letting go and trusting the process. I saw how gratitude opened my heart and I felt blessed in the highest realm. The presence of God is everywhere in the trees, the sky, the moon and everything. Then, in the darkness, came the most beautiful light shining so bright letting me know that God has arrived.

Love to all in this season
Love for no particular reason
Love means the real McCoy
Love is pure Joy
Love wakes up my heart
Love allows me to sing deep down apart

We Can Choose

There is sunshine up above although there may be
darkness down below. We must live in faith put our trust
in God's hands

There may be enemies amongst us but there may
be friendships close by. We must allow our hearts
to stay open

There are miracles happening every day there are disasters
on their way. We hold the key to open doors which can
give us what we need

There is heaven on Earth, there is hell within us
We can choose to see the light and let love shine

There is good luck around us, there is negativity in sight.
We have the power within us to change our lives

There is a God who created us, there is the Devil who
tempts us with our ego by his side. We are free to choose
our own path of true bliss

There is Peace in our hearts, there is hatred all around.
We can live in the moment and enjoy all we have
with gratitude

I am the One

I am a tree which is grounded
I am the air which I breathe
I am earth which I walk upon
I am a human soul which sings
I am a spirit who knows the higher realms
I am a drop of the ocean which is part of the earth
I am unknown to mankind which makes me unique
I am a masterpiece made by the hands of God
I am divinity in disguise which is connected to the source
I am a body which is only here for a short time
I am a successful woman who desires more

"To be at peace, surround yourself in nature."

"Love of self is the greatest gift you can give yourself."

"A loving heart is all you need."

"Faith in God and in yourself takes you to fulfill your life purpose with dedication and passion."

"You cannot give what you don't have, having love in your heart opens doors to greater opportunities to share your self-worth."

"I choose to enjoy the ride of my life as it is a gift."

"To love and accept yourself requires love and understanding."

"Be kind to yourself when times are hard."

"Only you can change yourself.
When you change, your world changes."

"True wisdom requires patience and being humble."

"Your greatest accomplishment is achieved when you are disciplined to be your best self."

"The beauty of life lies within us."

“A unique soul on this planet to make a difference.”

"Writer on my own journey, Lover of I,
Woman of greatness, Soul of Laughter,
Essence of God."

“I am my Own Sunshine.”

"Light up your life like there is no tomorrow."

CPSIA information can be obtained
at www.ICGtesting.com
Printed in the USA
BVHW042315290119
539019BV00010B/138/P

9 781912 551422